Out to Lunch

Out to Lunch

Andy Kissane

For Nick + Hilaire,
Here's to poetry.
warm wishes
Andy Kissane
Poetry Cafe 28·9·2012

PUNCHER & WATTMANN

First published in 2009

Published by Puncher and Wattmann
PO Box 441
Glebe NSW 2037

http://www.puncherandwattmann.com

puncherandwattmann@bigpond.com

National Library of Australia
Cataloguing-in-Publication entry:

Kissane, Andy

Out to Lunch
ISBN   9781921450204

I. Title.

A821.3

Cover design by Matthew Holt

Printed by McPhersons Printing Group

This project has been assisted by the
Australian Government through the
Australia Council, its arts funding and
advisory body.

for Freya

Contents

Loaves and Days

He throws the ball of dough
up above his head. His eyelids
are thick with broken sleep,
his hands white with flour. Lightning
hands. The rhythm in this tossing
and catching is mesmerising,
the unconsciousness of hands
that fling and pluck and fling again.
As if the precious organs of the body
have replaced the dough—a liver
striving for the ceiling, a kidney falling
to an open palm. A heart that is stretched,
kneaded and pumped, then plonked
on the waiting tray. Loaves edging forward
on rollers into a heat that will turn
sourdough golden and cook the crust
of the pumpernickel until it's as hard
as a fist. Loaves running together
like the hours and minutes spent
in the fluorescent glare of Gino's Bakery.
When he watches the last of them
slide away, he sees only bread,
not the tables they'll adorn like cut flowers,
not the man who never cuts an even slice,
or the woman who lifts up the rye
on a breadboard shaped like a bell.
He's had enough of this job, doesn't care
if he never bakes another loaf,
but he loves this moment
when he steps out of the furnace
into the cool darkness of a Petersham street,
runs his hand through his hair
and gazes up at the black wires
where the dawn birds line up,
fidgeting like choirboys about to sing.

Bus Ride with Grey Owl and Dancing Woman

I sit down the back of the bus and read,
This is all the Little Humming Bird is good for.
She goes about gathering husbands in strange villages,
until I am distracted by the woman in the plum shirt
with a Walkman pressed to her ear, dancing.
She shakes her body out into the aisle
and back towards the window so vigorously
that the man sitting next to her is forced to move.
This doesn't bother her in the least, this
is what she has been waiting for—now she can
really boogie—shoulders flung forward, head thrashing
with the beat and every now and then a sashay
to the side so she rocks for the passing traffic,
tongue rolling out of a wide open mouth.
Everyone on the bus watches
as she stands, shakes, bobs and grooves
to music that only she can hear.
We think she is crazy, but we tolerate her.
In the 1880s, women diagnosed with nymphomania
had ice applied to their vaginas, submitted
to the surgical removal of their ovaries.
I go back to the songs of the Tsimshian people
and when I look up, the dancing woman has gone.
The grey owl speaks in the dark of the evening.
Will you follow me through the hole in the sky?

Girl Reading a Letter at an Open Window

After Jan Vermeer

With both hands she holds the letter
and reads, the light of her youth shining
in the curtained room. Her eyelids appear
to be shut, as if she is contained
within her body, her love. Absorbed
in the fluttering page. I like the way Vermeer
has changed her stance, so she faces the open
window and is not, as her reflection suggests,
studying herself reading. She's not
in the room at all. She surveys
the chef's kitchen before ordering,
choosing a bowl of *banyas* and a tuna steak
seared on hot coals. Slices oranges
so the blood congeals on a silver knife.
Outside the Mediterranean washes
over black sands, goats pick their way
along hidden paths, their white beards
humorous and thick with salt. Her friend
says he would write her a love letter,
if he knew how. The creators of *SeaChange*
know that unresolved sexual tension
will maintain their ratings, just as Jane Austen
knew her novels should end and not begin
with marriage, and should contain a rake,
a rejected proposal and a young woman
who believes in her own cleverness. She reads
the letter again. Wouldn't you? The sun
spills onto her hands, while the words
take her out of the room and across the sea,
before sending her home again.
She is alive, but not a single scrap wiser
than if she had left the seal unbroken.
Who can resist such delicious fruit?

The Colour of Starvation

I cannot remember the details any more,
what it was that moved me. I was watching
this film in Year 11 at school, a documentary
set somewhere in Africa or India, where many people
were poor and starving. The film was long
and carried over into lunchtime when everyone else left,
except for a couple of do-gooders. Sucks, they called us.
I was so moved I went home that evening
and told my parents to sell their house so we could all
give up this life of decadence. Yet I'll be forty-five
in a month, and I am no closer to renouncing decadence.
Where has my idealism gone? And why,
like a jump cut in a movie, do I suddenly think
of William Morris, who said you could build a bonfire
with nine-tenths of a rich man's belongings.
Not that Morris was opposed to possessions.
He loved useful, decorative, beautifully made things.
He was only against the enjoyment of an object
that had been a pain and a grief for its maker to make.
Morris believed in the fulfillment of workers; he abhorred
the numbing boredom of the production line.
I see him wearing sabots and a smock, standing
next to the dyeing vat which is sunk into the earth.
He has mixed madder with wild mignonette, so his gold silk,
when laid out in a long, rich hank, has the captivating glow
of a sunset. Morris didn't like his colours to appear starved,
just as he hated the obscenity of starvation, recruiting
apprentices from the Industrial Home for Destitute Boys.
I don't know if he'd have stayed to the end of the film,
but I'm sure he'd have had something to say. For a long time
I've had this idea that I would write about a woman
with six children who works fourteen hours a day
in a factory with no windows. But what use would it be
if I managed to convey the tiring glare of fluorescent lights
and the nagging ache in her lower back? Or found words

to mimic the unceasing drone of the Singer—
twenty-four garments an hour, six days a week.
And what if, after labouring over the poem, I went to bed
with the contented weariness that comes from worrying over
the warp and weft of a single phrase? It's easy
to formulate the questions; much harder to live the answers.
Rising with the dew still on the windfall apples,
Morris eats five eggs for breakfast, dips his toast into his tea,
and looks out onto his garden city, the day already
stretching out as sunlight streams through the window.

The Festival of Kites

Everyone's on the roof.
The revellers' shadows ripple like saris
drying by the river. Two women sit
on the cool corrugated iron and watch
as a girl spins a stick, the mango-shaped
ball of twine working down to its seed.
On the other wall, a boy gazes after
the string, his heel lifting as if he might
step over the edge, his left side a perfect
fluid line, arm bent at the elbow,
the long dark fingers of his free hand
clutching at air. His face all innocence
and rapture. Above him the kite flares up,
becomes a white peacock strutting the sky.

Meat Matters

Forequarter Chops

You are routine.
Growing up
we ate you
every Tuesday night
along with mashed potatoes,
mint peas and diced carrots.

Now there's chump, loin and cutlets
for competition.
But back then
there was only
the ubiquitous forequarter—
burnt black
and dried out
under the gorilla.

Now I eat you
any night of the week,
barbequed, rare:
white bread soaks up the blood
and my teeth bite down
on a new idea of order.

Lamb's Fry and Bacon

You two go together
like Lillee & Thompson;
Simon & Garfunkel;
Starsky & Hutch.

After escaping
the hungry stare
of Leopold Bloom's cat,
the offal seems glad
to be sizzling in the pan;
the bacon crackles and bursts
like a drum solo.

Taken on your own
you're just OK—
like school—
but eaten together
you become
a woman in a ball gown,
a slipper that fits,
a fairytale ending.

Chilli Beef Stir Fry

Cats' tongues—
sweat behind the ears,
violent hiccups.

The Humble Sausage

I wandered lonely as a sausage
Without a slice of bread...

*

Shall I compare thee to a bratwurst roll?
One whiff of garlic and I lose control...

*

Sausage! Sausage! Flaming bright
On this sticky, summer night.
Your casing gapes; your insides burst—
If only I'd parboiled you first.

*

so much depends
upon

a red frank-
furt

squirted with tomato
sauce

lying in a
roll.

*

I will arise and go now, and go to the charcuterie.
Nine varieties they have there, of beef and lamb and pork.
I shall buy a dozen each—what joy, what glee
to see them browning in the pan, to pierce them with a fork.

*

In the room the women come and go
Munching on Cotechino.

*

But I see nothing, nothing... only sausages.
Five sausages. Five sausages in a tray.

*

Byron loved his mortadella
as much as any other fella.

*

Call me Chorizo.

Sunday Roast

Like a Christmas tree
I decorate you
with sea salt, garlic cloves, sprigs of rosemary.
A drizzle of olive oil.
The vegetables crowd around you
like spectators in the outer
crying carn, carn,
and chewy on your boot
you great big galoot.

You're one makeover that always fails.
Might as well just give Dad
the carving knife
and heat up the gravy.
O old friend,
you're as safe
as cricket on the radio
and naturally, you'll deny
until the cows come home
that a public servant
ever told you
that they did not, repeat did not
throw the children
overboard.

Pig's Trotters, No Kidding

One Easter in Akrata,
a small Greek village in the Peloponnese,
I befriended
three baby goats.
Each day I would go
out the back of the house
to feed them,
patting them and mooning over them
like a child
who has finally been given
the pet she longed for, begged for.
I was especially fond
of this black one
with a white blaze on his face
and white patches around his eyes.
As soon as I arrived,
he would come up to me
and nudge my chest,
searching my hands for grass
or food scraps.

One day I could only find
two kids in the enclosure
behind the shed. The black one,
my favourite, had gone.
When I asked where he was,
I was told that he'd been taken
up the mountain, to pasture.
I guess I believed the story.

Soon the night of prayer and feasting
was upon us. At the church
the priest sang the liturgy
in a monotonous tenor and the nun
we had christened Darth Vader

threw holy water in our faces. Outside,
firecrackers exploded in the square,
candles flickered in the night air
and everywhere I heard the greeting,
'*Christos Anesti!*'

Back at the house,
the table was laden with food
and a huge pot of boiled meat
bubbled on the stove.
It was 2 am. My hosts
served me some of the meat.
When I asked what it was
I was told—through a translation
that seemed far shorter
than my hosts' smiling, winking Greek—
that it was a dish of pigs' trotters,
a delicacy!

Somehow I was never
completely convinced,
but I ate the jellied hoof,
savouring its sticky richness,
holding the bone in my hands
and gnawing at the meat
until I had picked it clean.
To this day
I don't really know
if I ate pork or
the blessed hoof of my frisky friend.

Mincemeat

My mother used to
mince beef
on the green laminex kitchen table,
the silver mincer
mounted on a corner.
Sometimes I'd help by turning
the handle,
watching as the meat fell
into a yellow bowl—
long red strips marbled with white fat.
One evening,
when I was an ignorant twelve,
my mother wound the handle
of the grinder
while she simultaneously explained
the facts of life.
I cried—partly
at the shock of it all
and partly because of the shame
of being that old
and not understanding what everyone else
seemed to know already.
The mincer churned, then
my mother's floury hands
kneaded, pumped and pushed
the pastry,
before rolling it out
over greaseproof paper.

Joy and a Fibro Shack

*'I'm a little ashamed that I want to end this poem
singing...'*— Robert Hass

The difficulty of writing a poem
is like the difficulty of building a house
without a plan, wood, a hammer.
You have to start somewhere
and if you have a tin of nails,
then that's as good a place as any.
The foundations, the frame and the finish will come
if you work at it.
Or might not come.
There's always the canvas shell of a tent.
There's always driftwood and burlap fastened with bamboo vines.
There's always the music of corrugated iron in a hail storm,
or its blistering shade at midday.
Is a poem a palace or a humpy?
I prefer humpies, furnished with a daggy couch
reclaimed from the council clean-up.
I want to capture the grit beneath fingernails,
the mysterious gaze of a brush wattlebird
peering at me through the window,
the misery of a broken marriage,
and the elation of the night we bumped
into Rebecca at Kilimanjaro, the restaurant
not the mountain, crammed around a table
as those first contractions took hold of her body.
Breath, heartbeat, blood—the nervous dash
to the hospital. Then screams far too loud,
far too long for the sanitised labour
of soap opera—they'd call it over-acting,
they'd call it *amateur*, they'd say
it was in very bad taste.
I prefer poems to come into the world
shining with vernix, green with meconium,

radiant with the open-eyed awe of a baby
in the first half-hour of her life,
while the wind lifts and rattles the walls
until the house resonates with its own bright keening,
like the night I was up at 3am,
walking the kitchen, walking the hallway, walking
the lounge room, holding a baby
who would not stop, would not stop,
just would not stop crying.

Visiting Melbourne

'And then they called out your names...'
— 'Patchwork Quilt', Sweet Honey in the Rock

1

I stop. Someone has called out my name
with certainty and conviction. My birth
name, not the shortened version I now use.
How did he pick me out from the crowd
on Jolimont station? An eye for faces perhaps,
for the youthful grin lurking in my weathered chin.
An old school mate, excited to see me
after twenty-five years. And I him. My team

had beaten his, once again, but there's
no stirring now, nor any need to brag of goals
bagged from the boundary line. Instead, inevitably,
we talk of those we've seen, or still see, those
who have made it, and as rumour has it,
those who have died by their own hand.

2

Those who have died by their own hand.
The night air so cold we watch each other
breathe. Not completely surprising, but still
there's the shock of knowing someone
who wanted to die more than they wanted
to live. An outsider, an enigma, as we
all are, by degrees. No point shaking heads
or searching for words to make it easy.

Comfort comes most readily in the bright,
blue eyes of his own daughter, standing there
with a black and white scarf wrapped securely
around her neck. Or the photo of my girl
beaming from the window in my wallet.
May that never happen to our own pretty ones.

3

May that never happen to our own pretty ones.
Though they will grow old, as my parents have.
There's no way to avoid it. But at least our
children won't spend these precious years
learning to fire an AK-47, or grieving
for a brother whose unlucky, unsuspecting
foot kicked at an innocent patch of dried mud.
My daughter switches off Grandpa's football

on the radio, then turns on the TV. Told
not to, she does it again and Grandpa
slaps her across the back of the legs. Only
takes a moment, but the imprint of an angry
hand will burn on in our minds like
the orange and violet flash of an exploding mine.

4

The orange and violet flash of an exploding mine
would not even register in my father's occluded
right eye. He can see only darkness—
the result of a routine operation gone wrong.
He gazes at me out of his one good eye
like he does not know me, like I am
a stranger, not his beloved son. My daughter
needs to learn obedience, he says. He means

respect, I guess, that way of making others
feel relaxed, at home. If I talk any more,
I will surely say things I will regret,
I will tell him he just doesn't get it.
Yet even the blind Tiresias senses
the rider clinging to the bolting horse.

5

The rider clinging to the bolting horse
is my niece, Emma. But that's another story.
Horse mad, like my daughter, she drives us out
to the hunt club where her horse, Puzzle,
is recovering from a strained ligament.
We walk through the fields searching
for a quiet pony with a white blaze. He takes
the carrot in one gulp, then sniffs our pockets

for another. Soon my daughter is trotting
around the dressage ring, the pony's hooves
kicking up grey sand. Her back straight, rising
and falling, she smiles each time she passes me.
There's no point denying it, this feeling of
a hand opening up my flesh to graze my heart.

6

A hand opening up my flesh to graze my heart?
Whose hand? Whose heart? Some people
think that there isn't any self to speak of,
no rich inner life. Only stories borrowed
and stolen from others. Like the lines
of this poem, this diminished thing, remade
by fingers that can only grip a pen, sung
by lungs that never pause to think of breathing.

In *Collected Works*, that great Melbourne bookshop
of poetry and ideas, Kris tells me of his son's death
and how he now comes to work in order to
keep going. It's the routine that helps. Although
I'm surrounded by books stacked to the ceiling,
I mumble something pathetic; I don't know what to say.

7

I mumble something pathetic; I don't know what to say
to my parents. They want me to take some memento
from the family home, before it's sold, something
precious. But all I need is already inside me.
I'll have whatever Greg wants, I say, on purpose,
just to be difficult. The ship with billowing sails,
the brass fire-screen, the china dinner set locked
safely away in the crystal cabinet. At the airport

we hug goodbye, though there are many things
we don't say. Or can't. In the taxi I think
only of you, my week of sole parenting
now done with. Home again, the rain soaks
my hair, my fingers fumble with the keys, then
I stop. Someone's calling out my name.

Leaving Home

The oven door was permanently ajar,
hanging by its last hinge, when my mother
crossed the kitchen and planted a kiss
on my father's bristly cheek, just below

his grey-flecked, neatly squared sideburn.
She didn't say anything or look back
as the wire door slammed shut. Striding
calmly towards the oak tree, my mother

glanced at the clothes line spinning idly
in the breeze, smiled at the garden gnome
lounging by the pond, his fishing rod poised
above the lily pads. Free from the ache

of varicose veins, she climbed the tree.
'At last,' she said to herself, 'I have managed
to get my priorities right'—and with that
the feathers sprouted from her scapula

and her dentures dropped, orphan-like,
from her lips. High now, dangerously high,
she stretched out her supple wings
until they were as flat as an ironing board.

Sensing the far-off salty air, she hesitated
for a moment, then leapt into the wind. She circled
the house once, gliding over the FOR SALE sign
in the front yard as if she might just perch

there, before rising up again. My mother
felt her heart beat with wonder at the way
the rolling air held her aloft. Her nomadic eyes
scanned the darkening north and she flew away.

Like Birds in the Cage

I tell him what I think of him.

He's asleep on the floor in a pool of his own vomit.
It's the same shade of yellow that you get
in those packets of Dutch Curry & Rice soup
and the thought occurs to me, objectively,
dispassionately, as if I'm observing a centipede caught
in the middle of a burning log, trapped by the flames,
the thought occurs to me that he might choke
on his own vomit. So I tell him that too,
how it would be better if he choked on his own vomit
and I make no attempt to lift his head or wipe his face clean.

His snores are loud, mumbling like some two-stroke
motor, the sound that floated down the streets
of my childhood on hot summer days
when everyone's father was out cutting the lawn,
except mine, when everyone's father was out
in their white-ribbed singlets and faded shorts
with the elastic waist and the flap pocket at the front,
pushing the Victa back and forwards
across the pathetic squares of burnt turf,
this universe of couch. When everyone's father...

So I tell him what I think fathers should be
and how far he falls short of the mark,
how there's not one hair on his head
worthy of being called father, not the smallest clipping
from his filthy fingernails. It's then that I notice
the silence around me, the deathly quiet,
the stillness spreading from the makeshift stage
in the mess hall of the Mulawa Women's
Correctional Centre to the audience of prisoners,
because next to me on the wooden bench
is an inmate holding a knife to my throat.

Her face a mask of rage, determination
and complete absorption. All three at once,
mixed-up and tossed about like dough
in those bread machines, that you leave cold
in the morning only to return the same day
to a warm, perfectly-shaped loaf. Crusty. Yeasty.
The odour of fresh bread hanging about the house.
Like a promise or a gift. It's the mystery of theatre
that the inexpressible can take on substance.
Airy habitation and all that. The blade of the knife
pressing into my neck. What to say? What to do?

I try this. 'I can understand what you're feeling,
but if you'll just bear with me, things will change…'
Everyone else on stage, everyone watching, freezes.
I try to channel my terror into calmness,
into energy, to go with it rather than hide it.
To give the woman an opportunity to leave
without losing face. Without failing again.
Knowing how we all fail. Fathers…
mothers, lovers, friends.

I look into her eyes until she takes
the knife slowly away
and walks back to her seat in the audience.

The Light Fantastic

I prefer the travelling life,
lugging my camera and wet plates
through the shimmering heat,
stopping at the occasional homestead
to make portraits as endearing
as any artist can hope for. Of course,
any study is, in the end, a self-portrait
for those who know how to read it.
Take my controversial depiction of frontier
life. The background is dense rainforest—
trailing creepers and staghorn ferns
and although there's a sense of luxuriant growth,
the longer you look, the more the darkness
of the bush draws you in. At the centre
is a pioneer, his white shirt and trousers
brilliant against the receding blackness.
One hand grabs a naked aborigine by the hair,
the other hand raises a rifle,
as if he's about to swing the butt down
into the black man's jaw. And although
the aborigine is smaller, off balance,
almost subdued, his left arm holds a spear
that is surely capable of piercing
the white man's chest. You can imagine
what came before and what followed,
but the moment has its own logic.
Even though it was staged
and took four giggling attempts
to get right, the white man still appears
a little smug in his imminent victory.
But is it a victory? I have noticed how often
people's sympathy is with the hunted,
how the underdog's plight transcends
the intentions of my benefactors.
Some say I have recorded the very pulse

of the continent: diggers sluicing gravel,
a mother nursing her baby on a wide verandah,
the luminous expanse of a sandstone wall.
But I have learnt to treat praise with caution.
You know that photograph of a bush picnic?
You must know it. Men reclining on matting,
drinking beer from enamel cups, at home
like gentlemen relaxing in their club.
One man pouring, another lighting his pipe,
the third gazing into the distance.
Saddles tossed down, horses resting, a scented gum.
It brings immigrants here in their thousands.
People only see what they want to—
men in harmony with nature, an easy life.
Yet you have to see what isn't there.
The sun, flies you can never get rid of,
sheep blighted with ticks, drought, loneliness,
and that white-ant called debt.

The Eyes of a Dragon

The novelist tries again to imagine the scene.
She wants to evoke the heat, the drought,
the sudden panic. Breathe life into the blank page.
She wishes her writing would come more easily,
but it never does. Time to gee herself up,
close her eyes and begin. 1928. The soak
near Coniston Station. There'd be an old man,
she thinks, sitting by the charred fireplace.
Bearded dragon, he'd love to catch a dragon
and roast it slowly, eat it with nardoo damper
and pigweed. The others are talking about the trouble
with Marungali. Going over it all again.
That white bloke, Brooks, the one who hunts dingoes,
took Marungali for wife without permission or gifts.
So Bullfrog speared him. Of course. It was
just like Bullfrog. Bullfrog and Padirrka.
Now the two of them are hiding in the hills,
where they'll be safe. Something moves.
Is that my lizard over there? The old man
gets up and walks noiselessly into the mulga.
The others ignore him. Crouching behind
the dragon, he raises his nulla-nulla.
But he is too late. The novelist stops writing;
she shifts in her chair. She hears children playing,
an engine turning over, birds chattering, the sounds
of a suburban afternoon. She wants the old man to live.
She pleads with Constable William Murray, asking him
politely to lower his Martini-Henry Mark Two rifle,
to understand that the Warlpiri don't speak English,
to realise that he is an intruder on their land. But
she cannot rewrite history, though she badly wants to.
Murray grips the reins of his sorrel mare
with his left hand and shoots with his right.
The bare backs of fleeing women, gunsmoke
floating across his face. She cannot save the old man.

She squints into the sun with the eyes of a dragon.
Over there, sprawled on the red dirt, she watches
the dust settle on an old man's bleeding lips.

Refugee Hospital

It doesn't have to be this way,
the donor letter pleads—your help
could make a difference. Whatever.
I don't know why I volunteered.
And though I expected hardship,
I could never have imagined the frenzy.
The operating theatre is only a shed—
concrete floor, the ribs of the walls
exposed, a corrugated iron roof. Rain hammers
the roof with tropical force, small animals
scutter across it at night, the sun bears down
until sweat drops from my eyebrows,
my chin.

                'I love this work,' I tell
my husband on a satellite phone, staring up
into the night sky as if I might find his face there
among the visible stars. Around 3am,
the wounded arrive again. Woken by Watson,
I dress quickly and sort the critical into a rough
order. Serious knife wounds staunched by wads
of palm leaves. I begin with a young woman
who has abdominal lacerations as deep
as her village well. Who would do this
with a machete, I think, and why,
but I know now that such musing goes nowhere,
there's only the logic of the IV line,
the respirators, the cardiac monitor.
I clean the wound, clamp and tie off
a ruptured blood vessel and struggle to stop
the deluge. I think I'm done when a blood jet
hits my forehead with surprising force. It's
the sort of special effect you might laugh
at in a slasher movie.

I motion for back-up
and a nurse wipes the blood from my specs
while my fingers search for the culprit. Common
iliac vein, median sacral, the Arc of Riolan,
the inferior mesenteric branching
in my memory like a Dickensian plot,
all chance meetings and buried connections.
I find the vessel just in time, the bulldog clamp
as valuable as anaesthesia, as quick
as morphine. I make the repair.

Triage is overflowing and
I must move on. The nurse will stitch her up,
her family will have some relief, some joy.
Provided her family has survived.
A rooster is marketing an early dawn
as I assess the next patient, confident
in what my hands can accomplish
with a little experience, a little luck.
I slip on a pair of new gloves;
endorphins flood my mind with hope.

Falling through the Hoop

Picture this. A perfectly straight road, parched
fields, grazing sheep. Henry, relaxing
at a card table, a row of tinnies, a flagon
and a billy lined-up neatly before him,
thwacking flies with a folded newspaper.
Heinz lounging in the canoe,
dormant next to the wire fence.
Whenever a car approaches,
the street theatre begins: Henry swigs
from the flagon of claret, Heinz
paddles furiously, for all his life
as if he hopes to propel the sleek boat
through the roadside grass.
They watch as cars swerve, as drivers turn
in their seats, stunned by this apparition,
a puzzling pageant ten miles out of Yarrawonga.

Heinz had a fall away jumper
that always looked slightly different—
a feint with his head, a bum wriggle,
a capacity to hang in the air forever
or sling his shot like lightning,
then do a little war dance
around his opponent as the ball swished
the net without touching the ring.
Someone joked that his jump shot
was like the soup with the 57 varieties
and the name stuck.

These memories, these images that stay
with us. Is that all we have? An album
of polaroid stills, crisp as a keel
sliding downriver, the wash sweeping
to the banks. One man slammed on the brakes,
adjusted his wide-angle lens, cursed the light

and snapped the scene: Henry nonchalantly
opening the paper, Heinz grinning with all
the luxurious confidence of his eighteen years.
The random calculus of appearances.
Heinz was popular with girls, skinny-dipping
with Miranda at Elwood, then describing
the way the white caps frolicked about her
as her breasts bounced in the moonlight.
Leaving everything else to our imagination.
Character, myth, the whole graceful arc
of story is built from planks such as these,
slowly and relentlessly, even when
the story seems to meander, taking you
to a suspension bridge slung across a ravine,
when you're afraid of heights
and desperate to get to the other side.

I last saw Henry at Heinz's funeral.
Heinz hanged himself
a few years after that holiday,
looping his bootlaces over the hoop
in his backyard and kicking
the milk crate away. I don't know
why Heinz did it. First to slam dunk
the ball. First one, out in the car park
after the game, pashing on. The list
goes on, for as long as I care to write.
Those who appear to have
so much, have so little.

We sat there, at the wake, drinking
beer, trying to figure it out.
Some stories have the wrong endings.
There are explanations, sure. Details.
How the roof rack was slipping from the car,
how we unpacked everything onto the roadside,
how I returned to Yarrawonga to buy

the missing nut. But some moments
resist, no matter how you worry
at them, or pound them, they will not
answer, they will not come back.

I still have the photo I took,
red wine spilling over Henry's cheek,
Heinz smiling through the summer rain,
smiling as he powers on, biceps flexed,
his arms one with the wooden oar,
caught in the rhythm of his youth,
flowing into the stroke, in perpetual motion
yet going nowhere.

With the Sea in My Face

I surfed with Mike Horgan until he disappeared.
Those wild stories about what happened—
transformed into a dolphin, seduced by a mermaid,
kidnapped by a submarine. I'd guess he was taken
by a shark or struck down by an aneurysm,
his brain swamped by blood as the weed clung
to him and the king tides carried him out to sea.

I drive into the car park, get out and sit
on the bonnet. The waves roll in, long and straight
like freeways, the spray flies back from the lip
like a bridal train. On the sandhills the kangaroo grass
has another bad hair day—all spikes, all peroxide green.
Below me the beach is deserted, the wind blowing
from the north, offshore, the sun a good three hours
from its own slide into water.

I love the time before I hit the surf, how
I'm more alive in my routines—my hand
massaging the board, pores of wax rising
on the deck. Climbing into my wetsuit, drawing
the zip up my back with the ease of a contortionist,
then sand between my toes as I head down
to the water. The sheer pleasure of not hurrying,
the way that old barrels and hollow trees
come back to you and the best rides of your life
flow into one perfect wave and you're flashing
through the tube with dry hair, your body
yet to feel the relentless barrage of fresh powder.

I'd like to say that Mike is out there with me,
but he isn't. In reef break and point break,
in glassy peaks and dirty, angry chop,
I surf alone. I lift my chin into a southerly swell;
I work the wave while the wave works on me.
I'll be twenty-seven soon, shit that's old,
and the only thing I've taken to is surfing.

I'll leave you now with the memory of Mike Horgan,
call him what you will. He could easily be Jimmy Page,
Penny Foster, Andy Lim or Martin Pike. Or the one
they call Rhino, the one they call Slasher. I'll leave you
with the wind squalling off Voodoo, one Saturday
in September when I'd been out there all day.
This big set rose up, right out of the continental shelf
and I paddled wide and fast and caught it,
nothing special though, until the wave jacked suddenly,
giving me no time to think, no time to do anything
but rock forward onto my front foot and dig
the inside rail in. The thing just pitched
and the chamber was round, sparkling
and I crouched and held my line, dipping
my head into the water, until it spat me out.
The sun sang and glittered inside the tube
and I stepped out of my body
into the tough, exhilarating world of glass.

With Burning Lips

i.m. Marguerite McIntyre (1928-1993)

Out beyond the break the dark surfers bob and drift
with the swell, peering into the distance as if the next set
will bring the one wave worth waiting for.
I walk beside you on the sand, telling you about Kate,
why I don't want to marry her, trying to find the courage
to end it. Not wishing to hurt her that badly,
but knowing I can't put it off any longer. Is there anything
as valuable as a friend who will lay your feelings
out before you, like the line marking off the wet and dry sand?
It's possible to find an equation for the pattern the tide makes
and each tiny undulation is both predetermined
and unpredictable. The chaos of nature. Wind howls
around us, smoke rises from the coke smelter,
a container ship inches across the horizon.
You smile reassuringly and suggest fish and chips.
How lucky I am to know you. My aunt the nun.
Full of talk, unless you're in front of the TV, your gaze
fixed on the screen with all the inevitability of high tide.
'It's good catechetical material,' you explain and launch
into an inspired reading of the dullest Hollywood vehicle,
delivering the gospel according to the Sunday night movie.

*

A few years earlier, driving through a *barrio* in Lima,
I turn to the Columban priest I'm staying with and ask,
'What's that man carrying on his back?' Glimpsed
through the window, a sheet of thatching on his shoulders,
tilted at the sky. 'It's his house,' Tom Ryan replies.
The rubbish piled in the street, then burnt each night.
Raw sewage flowing down the dirt road as a man
carries his house up to the land invasion on the summit.

So rocky and barren it could be Golgotha. On Christmas Eve
the church is thrown into darkness. Not *Sendero Luminoso*
blowing up another power station, but a star and a candle
gliding down from the choir loft, gliding on fishing twine
until the star rests above the stable on the altar.
A boy's glorious soprano floats after the flame, soaring.
Frat atat tat, frat atat tat. Masked men from the *campo*
follow the star, streamers trailing out from their costumes,
boots thudding against the concrete floor. Dance of the Three
Wise Men. Then Joseph, Mary and the baby Jesus, bawling.
The liturgy continues, but Jesus will not stop howling,
so Joseph takes the baby from Mary, lifts up his gown
and raises the boy's head to the nipple. The first Joseph
to breastfeed in public—a miracle of casting.

Later that night, I lose Tom, visiting house after house,
kissing cheeks, sipping hot chocolate, dancing with Vivian,
an American aid worker. When Tom finally finds me
he is furious, frantic for my safety, ranting about 'that woman',
convinced she is a CIA informer, and much worse,
intent on luring priests away from their vocation.
Christmas Day in the Chapter House, I eat a Peruvian salad,
orange habaneros flaming in my throat, spot fires raging
in my mouth, radiant heat singeing my lips. The walls move
and I soar above the table in ecstasy. Like the first time
I made love. Ever since I've been trying to recapture
the intensity, a chilli freak longing for sweat behind my ears,
endorphins buzzing, that amber sun inside my head.

Lurigancho prison. Fed-up with the overcrowded conditions,
waiting years for trials while drug dealers buy freedom
in a week, a group of prisoners take three nuns
and a social worker hostage. After a day of negotiating,
the prisoners leave the grounds in an ambulance.
At the gates they're fired on from all sides. 'We were shooting
at the tyres,' the police say, but they're either very bad shots
or liars. Eight prisoners and one nun die. They drag the dead

and the half-dead by their ankles and pile them up.
Shirts and trousers soaked, blood congealing
around noses, blood dripping off feet. One man's groin
over another man's mouth. The asexual postures of the dead.
The gruesome wounds of terracotta Christs, lashed high
on their crosses in countless Latin American churches. Joan Sawyer,
the nun, hit by four bullets, one through the back of her neck.
We carry her coffin up Avenida Tupac Amaru, the cemetery
a good three hours march through the hot, stinking streets.
A huge procession of people chanting, '*Basta ya! Vida sí, muerte no!*'

*

I sit by your bed in St Vincent's hospital. Your skin yellow,
your eyes closed. If I'm lucky you will wake and speak to me.
You have given others ways of reading their lives, walking
with them as they stumble towards understanding.

According to the Enneagram, your redeemed totem
is an Irish setter, her coat sleek with warmth. I wonder
what film you would use to explain death.
'Cancer's a terrible thing,' you say, rolling your chin
awkwardly on the pillow. I would like to comfort
you, talk, but I can only sit. Your name like a flame
on my tongue. Sister Marguerite McIntyre.

Sometimes we choose our companions,
mentors, lovers—and sometimes we are picked up
and carried, turned over and over and dumped
in the sand. I like to remember that day. Not
the antiseptic odour of hospital corridors,
but the squawking of the bossy gull as he tries to hog
all the chips. The brilliant glow of my headlights
as I see you hesitate, look back at me and smile.

Happiness

Because on Sunday morning through the bedroom window
we saw six Rainbow Lorikeets
feasting on the blossom of the spindly fruit tree,
their brush-tipped tongues working down
into the open buds of the flowers, their red
and yellow breasts, their blue heads
suggesting the otherness of all creatures—

and because this morning
when I went into the study and lifted the blind,
I saw a pair of 'mostly gregarious' Bulbuls
on the branches right in front of me,
their black crests gelled into a punk cheekiness
suggesting the sameness of all creatures—

and because when I heard you coughing through the wall,
I remembered the other day at The Last Drop
when the coffees came with miniature teddy bear biscuits,
and you picked up your chocolate teddy with its one
missing leg and said, this is what
John Howard has done to our country
and we laughed, the six of us, glad
to be out and eating lunch.

One of the company, a writer, said
she couldn't write anything at the moment
because she was so happy,
despite the dreadful election result.
But happiness can push the pen as easily as misery.

You cough again and I recall how the scent
of your vanilla balm fills up the car,
I think of our daughter sitting on the fence
outside her classroom every Friday afternoon,
waiting for me to walk up, glance at my watch
and complain that they've rung the bell early again,
just so she can shake her head, grin
and scold me for being dependably, reliably late.

Jumping Waves

Holding her hand in mine
as the green water
builds and threatens to break

over us, is
as close as you can ever get
to feeling important.

We rise up and over
the lip, a pair of floating,
bobbing terns, celebrating

our achievement. Then
we search for signs of the next
wave's wobble and thrust—

the cool thrill of its charge coming
closer—ready
to be lifted up again.

Radiant Heat

Our fireplace is shrouded, the chimney
blows soot and smoke into the living room.
It's only rarely that you get to light
a fire, my pyromaniac, my love.
Rent a holiday shack in winter and you
are in your element. You gather twigs and small
stuff, scrunch up newspapers, stack the wood
crosshatched so it balances and rises
with raw-boned promise. You build a fire as
we once constructed tepees, pyramids, cathedrals.
Behind pot-bellied glass, surrounded by marble,
or out in the open, circled by stones.
Nothing can rival the fire you make yourself,
stoked and cared for as if a child, the flames
leaping and dancing over the logs
they invited to the party. Inevitably, the morning
chill delivers a mound of ash and dust,
but there's always the fury of a spot fire
in a eucalypt forest fanned by northerlies,
the fascination of staring into tessellated coals,
the pleasure of lighting it all over again.

The Earlwood-Bardwell Park Song Cycle

1

The long Holiday is over.
The summer of shorts and bare feet, of sunblock and zinc cream,
of finishing a book and picking up another and finishing it too, is gone.
The summer of the shaded verandah, drinking cold beer
at six o'clock while the children shower, is gone too.
The day of crumpled paper, presents and the big lunch is long gone,
and would not even be a memory but for the bill from Visa waiting
to be paid. The long Holiday is over. The I'm bored Holiday is over.
Vacation Care is done with, its passing loudly celebrated. On this new day
a bodiless CityRail voice apologises for any inconvenience caused.
Cars crawl past school gates like squadrons of worker ants; the children
primped, polished and belted down in the back. They are clean.
There will be just enough time to sneak in a quick kiss
behind the wall of F block, before the Holiday is lined up and forgotten.
The bells rings. It is 9 am.

2

The noise of turbo engines fills the blue sky. High up the blue
is dense and consistent, it needs no air-brushing, no touch up.
But lower down, at the height of roofs and trees, looking to Hurstville
or gazing to the mountains, a hessian-coloured tent of smog
hangs over the suburbs. You can't escape from it.
If you don't happen to notice it this morning—beautiful day,
Jeff says as you buy the Herald—you still have to breathe it in.
It's cars mostly. God Car, as Mundey calls it. The latest monument
to the automobile looms over Turella Park. Architect-designed,
with walls the shade of sandstone, as if it somehow hopes to merge
with the smog. Peregrine falcons circle the stack, a dark blur
against a windowless cliff-face. In the 60s the peregrine
was endangered, absorbing DDT from the rodents and small birds
they ate until they became infertile—laying eggs too soft
to make it. But now their shells are hard again; their young survive.

Like these two falcons who have already breakfasted:
a sudden breath-taking dive too fast for the human eye to follow,
and that was the last the poor mouse knew of life. Now
they are almost at rest, a long leisurely loop over the bush,
before climbing again, cart-wheeling, then tracing the last miles
of the Cooks River as it slithers and slides to the sea.

3

It is good to sit in The Lounge Room café on Friday mornings
and read the teams. For forty years you have been reading
the team as selected, like some farmer calling his cows in for milking.

Backs:	Johnson	Michael	White
Half-Backs:	Lappin	Leppitsch	Scott
Centres:	Akermanis	Voss	Pike

and so on, the names of people you have never met, and never
will meet, yet feel this close to, because you know their first names,
nicknames and can remember like it was yesterday the moment
Johnno came streaming through the corridor—five bounces,
or was it six—then let fly from beyond fifty and hit the post.
It might have been goal of the year if only he'd kicked straight.
Still, it's good to read their names again this Friday, good
to sit in The Lounge Room and sip the organic brew.
Smaller than most lounge rooms, a red couch lines one wall.
A drink fridge fills the other wall, leaving space for only
two tables, one by the window, one near the counter.
The smokers sit outside in the sun, oblivious to the petrol fumes,
the traffic. Around the corner at The Europa, at the Video Café,
and at Sabrina's French Bakery the people sit as if they
have no homes to go to, no work to do. The latté mob,
the cappuccino, flat white, short black, long black mob,
and those who knowingly order a macchiato and a glass of water,
then roll their own cigarette while the world rushes by.
When the coffee comes, the steam brushes your forehead,
the first mouthful is hot and bitter, just as you like it,
and you suddenly notice your heart—pa-thunk,
pa-thunk, pa-thunk—beating beneath your shirt.

4

Teenage girls dress to go down the street after school.
One ties a scarf stylishly over her hair, another puts on cork high heels.
Teenagers already moving in their own world: the place of Cool,
the place where you Do Stuff, the Knowing place shielded
and kept from adults who haven't a clue what it's like.
At Simply Souvlaki, teenage boys eat pita and chip sandwiches,
their hair gelled into echidna spikes, proudly sporting
an afternoon's stubble on their chins. Bags scattered, they crowd
around a table that already seems too small for them, giving
the impression that at any moment they might break out,
shatter and spin into a space big enough for their aspirations,
their tomorrows. All the places teenagers go to hang out,
to chill out. The Pashing Places. Though no teenager
would call Nannygoat Hill that. Windswept and lonely, high
above Wolli Creek, high above the silent valley, high above a train
rushing towards the airport—one train, at least, that hasn't been cancelled.
Standing on the rock shelf, this couple aren't thinking about the view
anyway, but about how to pretend they're exploring, casually,
just wandering, when she's really dreaming of the contours
of his mouth, and he's imagining the swirling rapids of her tongue,
the shut-eyed warm darkness of the Long Kiss that will never end.

5

Silence in Homer Street. No pedestrians, barely a passing car.
At four a.m. the streetlights burn for no-one, shedding kilowatt
after kilowatt of incandescent brightness onto a sea of dumb,
black bitumen. A blue Hyundai Excel stops outside the Wine
Emporium. A boy, no older than fifteen, gets out of the car,
a crowbar in his right hand. Craving another scrap of utopia,
he swings the crowbar hard, trying to break through this fucking
tough glass. Tiny diamonds shatter and fall, but the door holds.
He swings again. Again. Attempting to murder his reflection,
to cleave through the outline of his own shining skull.

Putting his shoulders into it, the diamonds leaking onto the footpath.
He is bent on entry, on feeding the screeching sirens in his head.
He doesn't see the passing car or hear the constable approaching.
But just in time he realises, turns to the stolen Excel, opens
the passenger door and slides inside. The constable, only
twenty himself, notices that the driver's window is a third
of the way down. He puts his arm in, attempts to open
the door. He knows this kid: DJ, a Marrickville boy.
But before he can lift the knob, the engine roars and the car
takes off. 'Stop!' the copper yells, 'Stop!' With his left arm
hooked over the window, he has suddenly become a stunt man.
And this is no movie. As the car accelerates, he is dragged,
his trousers ripping, a boot coming off. He fires his service revolver
at DJ. The car swerves and he is almost sandwiched by a passing
truck: his head a bowling ball rushing to the pins, his torso
an inflatable doll buffeted by the wind. But he survives,
the car dragging him forward, the wind making his eyes water.
Pain somewhere in his leg. Regaining his balance—desperate,
frightened—he fires again. Two shots. Finally, the car
jumps the gutter, his arm jerks out and he is thrown clear.
DJ has been hit: one bullet through the chest, puncturing a lung;
one bullet in the stomach; and one bullet through the groin,
severing a femoral artery. The clear precision of forensics
that tracks the journey of a simple bullet, knowing how
it rips and shreds and scars, but not how it lives on
in the consciousness of a man dragged towards his own
death, and who only has a moment, no time at all, in which
his mind, or his index finger, or his whole person—who
can say how it happens—decides to squeeze down on the trigger.

6

You go to the valley to escape from the sun,
to walk through the bush in the middle of the suburbs.
The road reservation, the steep cliffs working their own
green bans here, preserving flora that has scarcely changed
in six thousand years. In Girrahween Park the smooth-barked apple

is still home to the little red flying fox. Bloodwood and turpentine
shade the path, false sarsaparilla trails its purple buds,
coral fern and mat-rush fill the understorey. The children
run ahead—as if exploring—those words of conquest,
of newness and unease still unexpectedly dropping from our lips
like a branch from a widow's gum. The oldest girl plays
at tour guide, each clump of maidenhair fern, each burnt-out trunk
and hanging branch a scene from the Land of Princesses.
Water trickles down, collects in pools and trickles on to Wolli Creek.
A train rattles past unseen. A rosella rears up, up towards
Nannygoat Hill and that other world, while this place of animals,
plants and birds, this place of the lizard who scuttles
beneath bracken as we approach, remains strange and wonderful,
even to those who can name the life that surrounds them,
who walk through this silence that is full of sounds.

                              7

Our faces glowing with the faint blue light of the television.
The place of the Jason Recliner that keeps your feet up
and your back down. The bench where onions are chopped,
the cupped blue flame that warms the risotto, the small box
that pings and reminds you to ENJOY YOUR SOUP. The table
set in a fashion that discriminates against left-handedness.
The pen placed around the gas heater so the child can safely roam
while the fire flares brightly but never smokes. The book place
and the iddy-biddy light that gleams while your lover sleeps.
The long corridor used for indoor cricket and not much else.
The place of hot rainwater; the morning and evening mirror.
The neatly mowed lawn that uses more water, fertilizers,
fossil fuels, biocides and person-hours than any third world
agricultural resource. The place of the pillow where that other self
dreams of the long Holiday and the young woman with pigtails
who serves you coffee in her bra and knickers. The windless place,
free from UV rays and other people, where there are no tests

to pass, except the ones we endlessly set for ourselves.

8

Across the road a flock of ravens gathers in the highest tree.
They chant slogans at all who pass, imitating the call
of a man after a car has squashed his foot. Aack. Aack. Aack.
Turtle doves coo from the roof of the prominent white church
on the hill, the sort of Spanish mission architecture
you'd expect to see in South America. Down in the valley
a silvereye giggles, a firetail crunches seeds,
a pardalote hops about the doorway of her tunnel.
Three dusky moorhen float down the creek,
while a night heron sleeps in an overhanging tree,
happily dreaming of frogs. The white-plumed honeyeater
and the red wattlebird hang about the banksia,
ducking their heads down to bring forth the nectar.
Soon the talkback radio of birds will be in full flight
as they croon, coax and call out for the coming of dusk.
At the traffic lights a woman stands with a hand
to her ear clutching the new necessity, talking, always
connected, never alone. The light turns green
and she crosses the road, still talking into the air.

9

Perhaps it was the sheer cliff-faces, the hills and
escarpments, the grey rocks and bruised sandstone
that lured the Greeks here. In the Bardwell Valley
they build against rock walls these houses
that are forever threatening to float free.
Perhaps by throwing bricks high up into the air
they thought they might glimpse the Mediterranean again,
savour the diamonds glittering on a smooth blue sea.
In the dress circle streets—Hamilton, Kitchener,
Prince Edward, such English names—they buy up
the Californian bungalows, then knock them down.

Erect a double-storey block of concrete that runs
from fence to fence, a monument to ego, a temple
for those who treasure the finer things in life.
When you buy a home, do you buy a 'lifestyle'—
that word the real estate agents love? Or is home
something simpler, harder to define, like the moment
when you open the front door and see the lasiandra
on the porch, bought specially to sell your own
hidden treasure, and suddenly feel your heart leap
at the sight of the first winking purple bloom?

10

Always moving through the valley, always moving.
In cars, in buses and trains, sometimes on foot with the dog
leading. Or best of all on a bicycle, enjoying the track
that surges, loops and winds from Homebush Bay
to Botany Bay. Once you're in the seat and flowing
you don't have to think about pushing the pedals
and even gear changes take only a half-thought,
the thigh muscles registering a different pressure
as the bike rolls on. Past green fields that are mown
and watered for the crop of the small white ball
that is never harvested, the numbered flags
flapping in the Autumn breeze. Past the place
of the circus tent where elephants graze once a year
under electric power poles, just waiting for Jeffrey Smart
to notice them and put them in a painting.
Past the bloodwoods, ironbarks and swamp gums
planted by the Men of the Trees, where the water
occasionally falls from the racecourse sprinklers
and the Sprite bottles bob and float downstream
like teal ducks. That place where shopping trolleys rust
in the mud, where burnt-out cars pause on the banks
like reluctant swimmers, where hopeful fishermen
cast and stand, showing not the slightest scrap of concern

for the chemical residues lying in the belly of the mullet.
On you go, nervously, through the dog-off-the-leash place,
and the swinging toward sky place. Cup and Saucer Creek
trickles around the Greek retirement home to greet you,
and then suddenly you see the old boat harbour, the cormorants
gathered on the grassy headland like they're going to school,
the principal a wise old pelican, the white egret sauntering
over the mud flats like a teacher on yard duty longing
for the end of lunch time. Beneath the bridge where pigeons
line up on the wire fence and on to the rubbish bins
patrolled and pecked over by grey ibis. Around the bend
where you waterplaned once, losing your glasses in the puddles
beneath the paperbarks, hopelessly searching for fifteen minutes
until some kind man found them, your own eyes useless,
your face caked with blood and mud. Ah, the river, the river,
never the blue of those real estate photos, but sometimes
a swamp green, there where the cockatoos screech and circle
in the evenings, there below the shop of the caramel cone,
the macadamia cluster, the wattleseed truffle. Rats live
under this bridge, but you leave them behind, pedalling on
to the park named after the stately prime minister who told us
to maintain the rage, the park where the Arabs gather each year
for a festival, the women cooking flat bread and marinated meat
on barbeques, the children bouncing, falling and bouncing again
in a castle made out of air. Here they damned the river once,
then diverted it, but the old swamps are market gardens now.
This place where time seems to have stopped, where it's hard
to know what century you're in, where a Chinese man in a conical hat
pushes a wheelbarrow through the raised beds and a woman
kneels to pull out onion weed as the boats lull and drift in the canal.
The planes scoot in over the home of the Dragons, so low
that if you bounced off the handlebars, you might almost touch
a wheel or a wingtip. All of a sudden you remember
your smallness, how you are just one person cycling beside a river,
how thousands of years ago this bank lay beneath the sea.
You pass the old middens and the stencilled white feet
hidden by concrete, this place of kangaroo grass and lily bulbs,

all these places of the people who gave Gumbramorra Swamp
its name—the Gwiyagal people, who were here first and are still
here, who fished and lived and moved in this place, here.

11

Neon, halogen and fluorescent shine all over the valley.
The sky is dark, the Milky Way dim. The emu's head
nestles between the Pointers and the Cross, that
impenetrable cloud of dust and gas. Outside the RSL
the lime green neon road swirls onwards, forever onwards
into the valley of death. Inside, fairy lights cluster
over the rows of one-armed bandits promising easy money.
The Spanish Mission stands solid, yet ghostly on the hill,
as if to challenge everyone who passes—the church
of the Inquisition; the white lady who floats in the clouds
above the grotto, radiant, immovable, trapped in stained glass.
The glow of deserted shops spills out onto the footpath:
bridal gowns ablaze with beading, designer boots standing
in handfuls of hay, tubs of olives in the old art deco cinema
that's now a delicatessen. On the opposite hill, in Bardwell Park,
the street lights flicker like stars. The moon rises over the hills
of Marrickville, the moon of workers and mystics, the moon
of the tax return and the tax refund, the cadmium yellow moon
of homework and tears at bedtime. The moon of the coming
election, of palm tree and hoop pine, of all things passed and yet
to pass. Swaying peacefully in the water until a fish jumps
and the globe breaks, before forming again—the full moon
hanging in the dark sky and floating in the dark water.

The Carpet Weaver

Kashan, Iran

Every day Azra walked to her uncle's workshop
to weave rugs too precious to walk on. Carpets
destined for America or Paris, where they might

adorn polished floorboards or be proudly hung
on the wall of a billiard room. At seven Azra
learnt how to beat down the threads with a heavy

iron comb. At nine she graduated to the loom,
her long, nimble fingers tying the Senneh knot
as tight and as tiny as her uncle required.

You can learn the history of a tribe from rugs,
her uncle liked to say—their wars, their religion
and culture, even their decadence. All day

Azra bent over the loom, carrying a jumble
of colours and knots in her head. A prince
with a falcon clinging to his wrist, a tiger

stalking the spotted ibex. All day she laboured
in a windowless room that was hot, stuffy.
Sometimes the children's voices mingled

and pealed like goats' bells, sometimes
there was only the sound of their breathing,
the pliant silk, the wind made by the speed

of their fingers. Occasionally, a girl would brag
of her accomplishment and they'd count knots,
or race to tie off the last thread in the green eye

of a dragon. At eighteen the doctor tells Azra
that her pelvis is so small, so misshapen that it will
surely crush a baby's skull. When the time comes,

she must have a caesarian section. If only I could
get that far, she thinks, as she takes the bloodied
pad out of her underwear. Her weaving has led

to this, just as the path leads to the hammam,
the bazaar, the Mosque. Tonight Azra will cry
as she tells her husband that their boy—she

doesn't know why but she thinks of the baby
as a boy—is lost, like the last one. There will be
no turquoise gems, no new rug, no days

of sunlight and birdsong, no table laden
with food and refreshments. There will be
no need to count the weeks, no cause to stack

the swaddling cloths in a corner of their home.
There's no point trying again, she thinks, I am
as helpless as a silkworm boiled in its own cocoon.

Summer Stroll

After dinner we walk down to the beach
and up onto the rockshelf. It's a daily ritual,
a summer pleasure made possible by these long

twilights the farmers hate. Yesterday, a pair
of sooty oystercatchers patrolled the rocks,
while the boys searched the pools for starfish

and for those suckers that close their fronds
around your little finger with the gentle,
undiscriminating grip of a baby. Tonight,

the sky is the colour of a dolphin's arched
back, only glimpsed for a moment, out
beyond the breakers. Past the headland,

lightning sheets the sky with a bridal glow
and then the thunder follows: a train hurtling
into the station, everyone standing at the very

moment they realise that it will not stop.
My daughter runs ahead, hair flying out behind her
like the tail of a beloved horse—an appaloosa

mare or brindle stallion—her hoofs kicking
up sand as she jumps the creek and canters
towards the rocks. The storm's closer now,

trees bending and cracking, sand stinging ankles
and vaulting at eyes. We huddle together
beneath a feeble hill. I want to watch the lightning

strike the water. I want to feel the awe
surge up at this power, this brutal buffeting.
It would be reckless and foolish, but it's tempting.

The wind slaps at my cheeks, it threatens to pick
me up and throw me down. With my arm a shield,
I follow the others home, my daughter still leading.

Already I can taste it, another ritual, a cup clasped
in two hands, steam lifting to my flushed face,
the lamplight sprawling over an open book.

Out to Lunch

Drinking Coffee with Mandelstam

Osip Mandelstam wore dark sunglasses into the café,
glancing nervously back over his shoulder. He was off

caffeine, he announced, explaining that his stomach
wasn't the best, so I ordered potato bread and peppermint

tea for two. Good, simple food. Osip told me that what bugged
him most about his life was learning that the clown,

the Judas, who had betrayed him had actually murdered
the rhythm of his lines and didn't even get

how the hairs of Joseph Stalin's moustache could resemble
a cockroach. Osip lifted the bread slowly to his mouth,

as if he had learnt to savour every morsel. 'No-one
in Australia has ever died for poetry,' I said.

'Nothing's worth dying for,' he replied, as the steam
floated up from the rim of his cup. 'Just live, while you can.'

Hanging out with Atticus Finch

I thought a lemon, lime and bitters might be
Atticus's poison, but he'd winked at the bar girl

and tossed back a double whisky before we'd made
the time of day. Sure, he wore glasses and his hair

was gray at the temples, but his top button was undone,
his tie very loose and there was no sign of that vest.

'The damn trouble with Harper Lee,' he began
in an Alabama drawl that had charmed many

a judge and jury in its day, 'is that the woman
made me out to be some kind of saint. I told her

to leave in the scene where I got down and dirty
with Calpurnia up against the back fence, but she

wouldn't hear of it. "I won't let my characters dictate
to me," she said. "You two can hump the pailings

like bitches on heat if you want, but I won't
tell of it. Not on your life."' Atticus has had

more of a life than Harper ever dreamed of, I thought,
as I watched him scribble his mobile number onto the back

of a drink coaster and roll it towards the barmaid
like a man who has finally broken the shackles and is free.

Vanity Fair has *One* Word with Elizabeth Bennet

Our readers would like to know more about Mr Darcy.
Pemberley is charming at this time of year.

Is he a good kisser?
It wouldn't be at all prudent of me to respond.

But you're a woman of frank and honest disposition.
Quite.

So can you please enlighten us on this matter of interest?
I'm not sure that it would be proper or civil.

Is he an abominable kisser, then?
No, on the contrary.

So how would you describe his kisses, Lizzie?
Agreeable. Very agreeable.

Do go on.
I'm afraid I've already said far too much.

Agreeable and... Just one more word?
Wet.

Good. Now the tape's running. Just let yourself go, dear.
I am very sensible of the honour of your questions

and your interest is flattering to my husband and myself,
but on the subject of the kiss, I will remain forever silent.

Skipping Lectures with Raskolnikov

I choose a table in the centre of the café surrounded
by empty tables, for Raskolnikov has a dread

of overhearing conversations. He is as thin
as unleavened bread and sits down without

taking his coat off, despite the summer heat.
I'm disappointed because I'd hoped to examine

the loop sewn under his left armpit where he hid
the axe. I'd like to experience what it's like

to walk the streets while concealing a murder
weapon. I order a pot of Earl Grey tea to share

and raisin toast with thickly-spread butter. His
beautiful dark eyes stare at me. He can't seem

to sit still and gets up to leave five times before
the toast arrives. I tell him how university students

now congregate on Facebook, but he is suspicious
of fads and can't understand how they can take out loans

they don't have to pay back for years. He has
suddenly become garrulous, talking with his mouth

full and revealing that he never would have
gone through with it, but that Dostoevsky

needed a murder to make his novel work and
needed a novel to support his gambling habit.

Raskolnikov still seems famished and pale,
so I order another plate of raisin toast

and ask him about the cold of Siberia. His eyes
light up and he's off again, and the afternoon

opens out before us like the Russian steppes.
I have a lecture to give, I tell Raskolnikov,

but I'm hoping no one will notice, least of all
the students, if I don't bother to turn up.

Chewing the Fat with Captain Ahab

Given my arthritic leg and the untimely disappearance
of his leg into the belly of Moby-Dick, vanishing

as quickly as champagne at a wedding, I thought
I'd have something in common with Captain Ahab,

that we might see eye to eye. But he is, to put it
mildly, a difficult man, only agreeing to meet me

on North Head on a day when a southerly buster
is blowing and the sea's littered with sullen surf.

Hardly the weather for a picnic. At first, I can't
find him anywhere, though I can sense his presence.

Occasionally I think I hear the words 'Avast'
and 'Flukes! man' floating on the wind. Finally

I find him, hoisted three-quarters of the way
up a Norfolk pine, staring out to sea. We

exchange greetings and I watch him swing
down from branch to branch with nonchalant ease.

I've already spread out the picnic rug and unpacked
the pickled herring and the beef jerky, but Ahab

isn't the least bit interested in eating, discussing fanaticism,
or ruminating on the parlous state of commercial whaling

in every country except Japan. He sways on the edge
of the cliff, balancing on his ivory leg, muttering

about a snow-white forehead and a speckled hump.
As far as I know, he's still there now, trying

to comprehend hate, the inscrutable sinew
and blubber of it, the rows of white teeth,

the open jaw floating up to meet him. His gaze
is so intense, as if he's staring down

the sun, but I can't imagine his face shining,
lit by the warm radiance of a smile.

Sipping Chardonnay with the Fallen Women

I'm out to lunch with Anna Karenina, Emma
Bovary and Tess Durbeyfield (who has shunned

aristocratic airs and wants no mention made
of the d'Urbervilles). They're onto their second

bottle of chardonnay and I can't seem to get
a word in. Of course, the word that's closest

to my lips is cleavage, and I'm doing my best
not to say it, or think it, by controlling the vectors

of my male gaze, and by trying hard to maintain eye
contact. Of course, my poems have always

been full of references to breasts, and to food,
which amounts to the same thing if your

a Freudian. Of course, it's you're before the slip,
which is now commonplace, as hardly anyone

these days knows what to do with an apostrophe,
or where to put it. I arrived early, in time to notice

the strange lightness in Anna's step, the upward lift
in the middle of Tess's top lip that makes her

so imperfectly beautiful, and the odour of sap
and verdure clinging to Emma's pale white skin,

her dishevelled hair. I sit and listen. Occasionally
I have something to say when the conversation turns

to glass ceilings, date rape, or the fact that Madonna
is now a rock star. But they are cool and self-sufficient

and they get on famously, like sisters, like faithful
friends, like women who know that the world

is theirs and that no man can deny, reject or
betray them again. They're free to do as

they wish, lunch as long as they like and drink
a third bottle of chardonnay whenever they want to.

Notes and Sources

Bus Ride with Grey Owl and Dancing Woman
The lines in italics are from *Song of the Sky: Versions of Native American Song-Poems* by Brian Swann (University of Massachusetts Press, 1993) pp. 60-61, 81.

Visiting Melbourne
I want to acknowledge my debt to Martin Langford's fine poem 'Aussie', published in *The Great Wall of Instinct* (Island Press, 1993), which gave me the idea for the last line of 5 and the beginning of 6.

The Light Fantastic
The photograph of the pioneer and the Aborigine was originally published as a postcard, photographer unknown, no date, Mitchell Library, Small Picture File/Taree Photographics and is reprinted in *Australia: Image of a Nation 1850-1950* by David Moore and Rodney Hall (Collins, 1983) pp. 42-43. The photograph of the bush picnic is by Richard Daintree, 'Bush Travellers, Queensland.' c. 1864-1870, National Library of Australia, Canberra and is reprinted in *Shades of Light: Photography and Australia 1839-1988* by Gael Newton (Collins, 1988) pp. 46-47.

Refugee Hospital
This poem was inspired by John Murray's story 'Watson and the Shark' published in *A Few Short Notes on Tropical Butterflies* (Penguin, 2004).

Happiness
This poem was written in response to, and shares some similarities with, Robert Hass's poem of the same title, published in *Sun Under Wood* (Ecco Press, 1996).

The Earlwood-Bardwell Park Song Cycle
This sequence was initially prompted by Les Murray's poem 'The Buladelah-Taree Holiday Song Cycle', which is itself a response to the Aboriginal sequence, 'Song-Cycle of the Moon Bone'. I am indebted to both poems.

The Carpet Weaver

The poem was inspired by Meg Mullins's story 'The Rug' published in *The Best American Short Stories 2002*, (Ed. Sue Miller. Houghton Miflin, 2002). 'The Rug' suggested the detail of child labour leading to a misshapen pelvis and repeated miscarriages.

Acknowledgments

Grateful acknowledgment is made to the editors of the following publications in which many of these poems first appeared, sometimes in slightly different forms:

Ask the Rain (Poets Union Anthology 2004*), Antipodes, The Best Australian Poems 2004, The Best Australian Poems 2005, The Best Australian Poems 2006, The Best Australian Poetry 2006, Blue Dog, The Cool Breath Burn* (Newcastle Poetry Prize Anthology 2004), *English @ Eleven: VCE English, Famous Reporter, From the Anabranch* (Poets Union Anthology 2002), *Griffith Review, Island, Light on Don Bank, Meanjin, Overland, Quadrant, small packages, Southerly* and *Wagtail.*

'Joy and a Fibro Shack' was a joint winner of the 1999 John Shaw Neilson Poetry Award.
'Falling through the Hoop', 'With the Sea in my Face' and 'With Burning Lips' were awarded third place in the 2001 Somerset National Poetry Prize.
'Loaves and Days' was highly commended in the 2002 Broadway Poetry Prize.
'The Carpet Weaver' won second prize in the 2004 Tom Collins Poetry Prize.
'The Earlwood-Bardwell Park Song Cycle' was short-listed in the 2004 Newcastle Poetry Prize.

I'd like to thank the Literature Board of the Australia Council for the Arts for their generous assistance in the writing of this book.